THE *OFFICIAL GUIDE* TO THE *CARTOON CLASSIC*

BY DANNY GRAYDON

RUNNING PRESS
PHILADELPHIA · LONDON

GEORGE

ELROY

Contents

INTRODUCTION 8

MEET THE JETSONS 14

THE LOOK OF THE FUTURE 38

A HARD DAY'S WORK 46

CUTTING-EDGE TECHNOLOGY 54

FAVORITE EPISODES, SPECIALS,
AND THE BIG SCREEN 62

POP-CULTURE FAMILY 74

CREDITS 80

INTRODUCTION

Original character sketches for Judy,
George, and Jane.

THE FAMILY OF THE FUTURE

Well into the far-flung future of the twenty-first century (2062, to be exact) live the Jetsons, a nuclear family consisting of a mother (Jane), father (George), daughter (Judy), and son (Elroy).

Theirs is a typical home in an automated society where virtually anything can be done with the push of a button. Residents of Earth live and work in space-age-style buildings in the sky and commute in flying capsule cars. They ride on moving sidewalks and lounge as sliding chairs deliver them to their destination. Vacationers spend time at Las Venus and Moonhattan. Robots and specialized gadgets take care of all menial tasks. Household machines automatically clean, cook, scan, brush, fluff, coif, rearrange, transport, transmit, remind, and locate.

These devices also tend to put their human users in odd and often hilarious situations. For instance, a person may get a mouthful of shaving cream or a bizarre hairdo if he or she pushes the wrong button during morning grooming. In the Jetsons' world, too, the robots are apt to respond with smart-aleck attitudes, be snoopy tattletales, or simply short-circuit at inappropriate times.

Despite its sci-fi whimsy, *The Jetsons* is, at its core, the story of a typical sitcom family and the wacky situations its family members find themselves in. The characters are delightful, viewers can relate to them, and they have proven themselves to be very enduring. They may well still be on television when 2062 rolls around.

THE BEGINNING OF 2062

If it weren't for the massive success of *The Flintstones*, *The Jetsons* might never have been. "It's not particularly brainy to say, 'Well, with the Stone Age here, let's go into the future there,'" Joe Barbera recalled in 1997, but, he added, "we started with that basis." *The Jetsons* was hardly just an update of *The Flintstones*, however. A lot of thought went into how the passage of time would affect family life, and the dynamic of *The Jetsons* is markedly different from that of their Stone Age counterparts.

The artists working on the series faced many questions as they got to work. What could the future look like? How would things interact in the future? What could be easily exploited, hyperbolized, and utilized for full cartoon effect?

Though the futuristic backdrop was populated with aliens, holograms, elaborate robotic contraptions, and other whimsical inventions designed to make life easier, the characters still (amusingly and humanly) complained about the remaining inconveniences. *The Jetsons*, like *The Flintstones*, was firmly anchored by a tendency to present recognizable contemporary situations in its distinct setting.

Unlike the Flintstone family, whose patriarch Fred worked a blue collar job, the Jetsons were firmly middle class. George Jetson was conceived of as a corporate employee who, along with his homemaker wife Jane, would be a parent to two children. Their eldest, Judy, was a teen-age girl whose presence catered to a growing teen culture. Their youngest, Elroy, was smart, sweet, and well mannered despite his impish appearance. At the time of the *Jetsons* premiere, there were not yet any children on *The Flintstones*. The "birth" of Pebbles Flintstone actually occurred while *The Jetsons* was in its first season. However, even when Pebbles and her friend Bamm-Bamm Rubble became regulars on the series, there was still a significant difference between how the two shows integrated these young characters: The relative maturity of the Jetson children meant that they were able to fully participate in each episode's plot.

Original designs for Elroy Jetson. Hanna-Barbera artists considered giving Elroy eyes with pupils (far left) before settling on the twin black dots that distinguish him from the other main characters in the series.

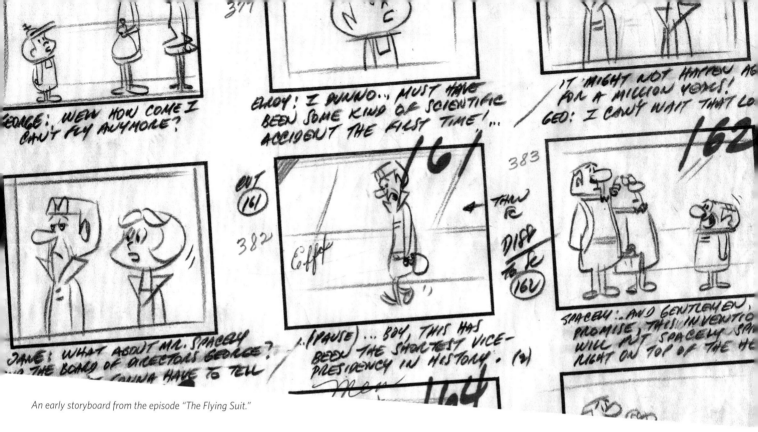

An early storyboard from the episode "The Flying Suit."

The first episode of *The Jetsons* immediately thrust audiences into the show's wondrous future. There was TV's newest cartoon family speeding through the skies above Orbit City in a bubble-topped capsule car. The opening story was classic sitcom territory, as the Jetsons welcome Rosey the Robot Maid into their home, where she promptly wreaks havoc when George's boss, the blustery Mr. Spacely, comes to visit.

AMERICA LOVES THE JETSONS

The unique futuristic setting of *The Jetsons* was an instant hit with TV viewers. Audiences could gaze in wonder at a stylish landscape of suspended buildings, space-age furniture, and near-infinite technological conveniences, while still getting in plenty of some-things-never-change laughs. Many of the show's plot elements, such as George's wranglings with his totally unreasonable boss and Judy's teenage mood swings, were just as likely to occur in 2062—and maybe even in 3062—as in 1962. Like *The Flintstones*, the show had a timeless appeal, and though its original run included only a fraction of the number of *Flintstones* episodes, the series enjoyed an impressively lengthy life in syndication and a second season twenty years after the first. Additionally, the extensive merchandising of *The Jetsons* helped it stay in the pop-culture consciousness. Today, the original episodes are rightfully regarded with huge affection.

GEORGE

JANE

ROSEY

MEET THE JETSONS

GEORGE JETSON

George Jetson is a bumbling yet lovable family man and—so he thinks, anyway—an industrious working professional. Audiences sympathize with, laugh with, and ultimately adore him. He has a tendency to put his foot in his mouth and often exclaims "Hooba-dooba-dooba!" when surprised.

Although George clearly loves his wife and kids, he may quickly say no to their requests—an action he usually regrets. He adores his wife and indulges *most* of her wishes (there are notable exceptions). As a doting father to Judy, he usually disapproves of her active social calendar and her choice in boyfriends. He also keeps a firm hand on young Elroy so the boy won't stay up past his bedtime, walk in the house with moonshoes on, or choose an inappropriate TV show to watch. George also shares a special bond with the family dog, Astro, but when the canine needs a walk on the treadmill, George may be too exhausted from his three-hour workday.

Yes, George works a punishing full-time schedule of three hours a day, three days a week, as a digital-index operator at Spacely Space Sprockets. There, George is downright meek, because his domineering boss, Cosmo S. Spacely, constantly antagonizes him, making George wish he had better excuses and more profitable ideas. Though he's often lazy at the office (when he manages to get there on time), George believes he deserves a raise and a promotion to vice president. Unfortunately, Spacely knows how much he craves the promotion and loves to dangle it over his head.

Though likely to get plopped into the midst of precarious and confusing situations, George always sees the error of his ways and does the right thing in the end.

Q GEORGE IS SHOWN SCREAMING, "JANE, STOP THIS CRAZY THING!" IN THE CLOSING CREDITS OF EACH EPISODE, BUT WHAT EPISODE IS THE LINE ORIGINALLY FROM? **A** "MILLIONAIRE ASTRO"

About George

AGE Mid-thirties (exact age unknown)

HAIR COLOR Red

OCCUPATION Digital-index operator at Spacely Space Sprockets

TRIVIA George doesn't eat bananas

ORIGINAL VOICE ACTOR George O'Hanlon

Q WHEN IS GEORGE AND JANE'S WEDDING ANNIVERSARY?

A JUNE 2

3 Facts about George

1. George's boss, Mr. Spacely, has been torturing him ever since they were children and George ran Spacely's lemonade stand.

2. George doesn't start work until 11 a.m., yet still has trouble getting there on time.

3. Though his day job is at Spacely Space Sprockets, George is an accomplished drummer and performs an amazing solo during the episode "A Date with Jet Screamer."

JANE JETSON

Jane Jetson is a devoted and caring wife and mother whose even-tempered personality provides some relief in the hectic Jetson household. Jane, who likes to discuss family matters with George, is the perfect foil for her husband, demonstrating calm, reasonable responses to his over-the-top tirades. When George is perched on the precipice of disaster, Jane usually comes to his aid.

Jane is always happy to see her kids having fun. She likes Judy to have a full social life and enjoys their girl-talk sessions. Jane also exudes a cheerful air with Elroy. All the while, she still commands a supervisory role—expecting the kids home for dinner, doling out warm clothes on chilly winter days, and making sure they do their homework.

Though the Jetson family's ultramodern automated pad requires little maintenance beyond pushing three buttons to vacuum, iron, and do the wash, Jane finds housework tiring and hires a robot maid.

She has a passion for fashion and is always searching for a new look. And while she's not as prone to disasters as her husband, she still manages to land in futuristic, far-out situations— just like the rest of the family.

"Elroy's TV Show"

3 Facts about Jane

1. Jane met her husband George when he crash-landed on her patio.

2. Jane was once diagnosed with "buttonitis," a malady caused by pushing too many buttons.

3. Mooning Dales is Jane's favorite store.

"Elroy's TV Show"

"Rosey's Boyfriend"

About Jane

AGE 33

HAIR COLOR Orange

OCCUPATION Homemaker

TRIVIA Jane briefly held the title of Miss Solar System

ORIGINAL VOICE ACTOR Penny Singleton

Q WHAT IS GEORGE AND JANE'S SONG?
A "SATURN DOLL"

JUDY JETSON

Judy Jetson is a bubbly, kind, fun-loving, typical teenage girl. Her trademark ditsy, excitable behavior is very appealing—and a hoot to watch. Judy genuinely loves her family and gets along well with everyone most of the time. She is usually respectful of her parents and nice to her little brother, Elroy. As with many adolescents, though, Judy's mood can quickly change from blissful to despairing, and her greatest concern is her whirling social life.

She shuns schoolwork in favor of rearranging her room and swooning over rock stars. Judy, who always wants to go along with the crowd and is crazy over the latest fads, loves to shop at Laser's department store and would like nothing more than to own a Moonserati sports car so she can impress boys. But she goes through boyfriends so fast that not even Rosey can keep track of them. Judy runs her life to the letter as dictated by her microprocessor personal organizer and diligently records all her precious secrets in her digital diary.

"Elroy's Pal"

3 Facts about Judy

1 Some of Judy's past boyfriends include Buddy Blastoff, Harvey Sonicblast, Eddie Rocketowski, Johnny Moonigan, and Ricky Retro.

2 Judy attends Orbit High School.

3 When George can't take Judy to the Father-Daughter Dance, she's relieved because dad can't dance. But then she finds out Grandpa Montague Jetson will take George's place!

"Jane's Driving Lesson"

"Rosey's Boyfriend"

About Judy

AGE 15

HAIR COLOR White

OCCUPATION High school student and occasional songwriter

TRIVIA Judy enjoys space skiing

ORIGINAL VOICE ACTOR Janet Waldo

Q WHAT SUBJECTS DOES JUDY STUDY?

A CYBORG BIOLOGY AND ASTRO MATHEMATICS

ELROY JETSON

Elroy Jetson is a brilliant, chipper, outgoing, pint-size boy. He doesn't mind school, but he also likes sports, playing with friends, and other regular kid pastimes. Like many children, he worships TV superheroes, invents secret codes with his pals, and plays with toys in the house.

Elroy, as a child of the future, enjoys splitting atoms, trying to invent flying pills, chatting on his intergalactic two-way radio, and having a talking dog and a furry alien as pets. Being both a slightly adventurous kid and the son of George Jetson, Elroy finds himself easily propelled into outrageous situations, managing always to catch a little luck to help him out.

Q WHAT IS ELROY'S SPACE CUB TROOP NUMBER?
A TROOP 54

"The Coming of Astro"

"A Date with Jet Screamer"

"Rosey's Boyfriend"

"Elroy's Pal"

About Elroy

AGE 6 ½

HAIR COLOR Yellow

OCCUPATION Elementary school student

TRIVIA Elroy wants to be a scientist when he grows up.

ORIGINAL VOICE ACTOR Daws Butler

3 Facts about Elroy

1 Elroy attends the Little Dipper School, where he is a straight-A student (according to his report tapes).

2 In the episode "Elroy's TV Show," when Elroy becomes the star of the television show *The Adventures of Spaceboy Zoom and His Dog, Astro*, he makes a weekly salary of $5,000.

3 Elroy plays "left sky" for his spaceball team, the Space Cubs, which is part of the Little Dipper League.

ASTRO

Astro is the Jetsons's loopy, affectionate, very large talking dog. Like most dogs, Astro only wants to please. He craves love, fun, food, and the chance to sleep inside.

Only Astro's heart looms bigger than he does. He loves his family, especially George. When George is near, Astro, angling for a canine snuggle, often throws his huge forepaw around George's shoulder. George finds this Astro practice—along with his gooey kisses—annoying. And because Astro's dog heart is big, it easily breaks. If George doesn't give him constant love and attention, Astro will burst into tears and believe no one loves him. George frequently finds himself apologizing and succumbing to Astro's sweetly clumsy, often-cloying, talking-dog needs.

For all his huge, furry mass, though, Astro appears to be void of even one slobbery ounce of bravery. Meek and gentle, he runs scared from dangerous situations.

Astro's ability to talk, his limitless affection for George, and his oafish, endearing personality make him an integral part of the Jetsons's loony life.

About Astro

AGE 5 (35 in dog years)

FUR COLOR Gray with white muzzle

OCCUPATION Family pet

TRIVIA Before coming to live with the Jetsons, Astro was owned by zillionaire J. P. Gottrockets

ORIGINAL VOICE ACTOR Don Messick

ORBITTY

O rbitty, an adorable little furry alien who serves as a pet for the Jetsons and as Elroy's sidekick, was introduced during the second season of *The Jetsons*, when Elroy found him on a school field trip to an alien planet and brought him home. Orbitty has spring-like legs with suction cup feet and is fond of purring, whistling, and changing colors.

Though closer to Elroy than anyone else, Orbitty will go out of the way to help any Jetson family member— even Astro, who was originally very jealous of Orbitty.

About Orbitty

AGE Unknown

HAIR COLOR White and purple

OCCUPATION Family pet

TRIVIA Orbitty changes color according to his mood

ORIGINAL VOICE ACTOR Frank Welker

Pink = affectionate

Yellow = scared

White = neutral

ROSEY THE ROBOT

Rosey, the antiquated, spunky, emotional robot maid that keeps the Jetson household in order, tries her hardest to be a helping hand. Though supposedly outdated, Rosey is quite multifunctional: She can process Judy's homework tapes, teach Elroy how to throw a tight spiral football, and turn messy leftovers into a five-star meal. Rosey also has spiffy transformer capabilities in her arms and hands that allow her to instantly produce whistles, massage rollers, cigarette lighters, and any other items someone may need.

Just as quirky as the rest of the family, Rosey stands as a rather imposing family member and will not tolerate back talk. She originally came to the Jetsons via a one-day free trial, during which she told off Mr. Spacely and dumped a pineapple upside down cake on his head. Though supposedly not wired for emotion, Rosey ends up falling in mad robot love with the local robotic handyman.

Rosey's blunt wit, sassy attitude, old circuits, and unconditional love for the Jetson family add a nifty twist to every tangled story.

About Rosey

AGE Rosey prefers to leave her age out of it

BODY COLOR Blue

OCCUPATION Maid for the Jetson family

TRIVIA Rosey came to the Jetson home from U-RENT-A-MAID

ORIGINAL VOICE ACTOR Jean Vander Pyl

THE LOOK OF THE FUTURE

An original layout sketch of Spacely Sprockets.

Mid-21ˢᵗ-Century Modern

The *Jetsons* has one of the most distinct looks in all of cartoonland. The artists at Hanna-Barbera drew from modern architecture—in particular, the work of architect Oscar Niemeyer—while adding their own unique touches. They imagined (quite rightly) that parking and pollution would be a problem in the future and thought of unique solutions to both: Buildings rear up high enough into the sky to avoid unfavorable atmospheric conditions, while capsule cars fold up into neat suitcases. Stylistically, the show referenced the popular and vividly expressive Googie architecture of the period, with the sky-high setting giving it a new twist. The artists also drew from futurist books such as *1975: And the Changes to Come*.

An early sketch of Elroy Jetson.

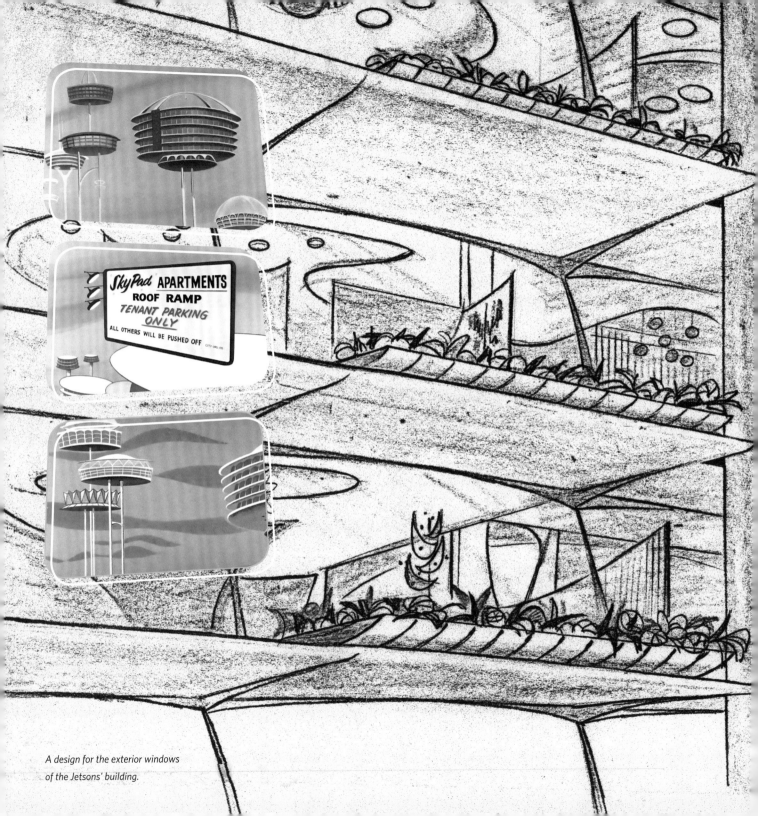

SkyPad APARTMENTS
ROOF RAMP
TENANT PARKING
ONLY
ALL OTHERS WILL BE PUSHED OFF   CITY ORD. 170

A design for the exterior windows
of the Jetsons' building.

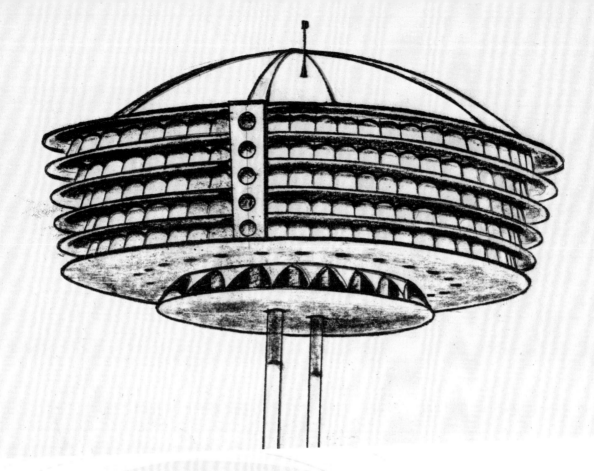

SkyPad Apartments

To say that the Jetson family lives in a high rise is an understatement. Hovering on the skyline, the building is capable of traveling high enough to avoid inclement weather with only the push of a button.

The Jetsons share the building with 1,999 other tenants. In the episode "Uniblab," it's revealed that they live in Apartment 104, although this number never appears on the door in any other episode. Usually, their door is blank, although sometimes "Jetson" is written on the outside.

The inside of the Jetson's three-bedroom apartment is furnished with sleek, modern furniture and the latest home appliances. Should they want something different, redecorating is as easy as flipping a switch. In the episode "The Coming of Astro," Judy instantly changes the look of her bedroom from "Space Provincial" to "Moon Modern."

Sally's Satellite Dress Shoppe

Spacey's Department Store

Universal Travel Service

A sketch of the barber shop where George gets his hair cut in the episode "Jane's Driving Lesson."

30 Second Cleaners

Businesses

The Jetsons frequent a variety of businesses that offer the latest in 21st Century amenities, from 30-second dry cleaning services in "The Flying Suit" to a customizable hair-styling helmet used at the barbershop in "Jane's Driving Lesson."

Las Venus Venus

Riviera Satellite

Flamoongo

Supersonic Sands

Las Venus

George and and Jane's second honeymoon at Las Venus allowed the artists at Hanna-Barbera to create a futuristic spoof of Las Vegas and its iconic architecture and amusements. While the Sonic Sahara and the Supersonic Sands, where the Jetsons stay, are reminiscent of actual Vegas buildings, the Las Venus Venus has a facade that looks like a giant set of dice, the Riviera Satellite resembles a slot machine, the Flamoongo is a giant roulette wheel, and the Supersonic Sands is modeled on a stack of poker chips.

A preliminary sketch of the Super Sonic Club, where George and Jane dine in the episode "Las Venus."

A sketch of George in his office. Note the color references and instructions for the animators.

"Private Property"

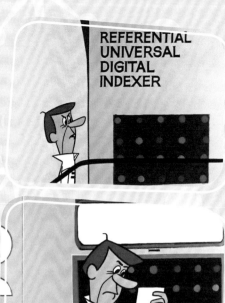

REFERENTIAL
UNIVERSAL
DIGITAL
INDEXER

"The Good Little Scouts"

Workin' 11 To 3

George Jetson works hard at Spacely Space Sprockets. *Really* hard. He has a grueling full-time schedule of three hours a day, three days a week—starting at 11 a.m. and ending at 3 p.m. (with an hour for lunch).

Though he's on a constant quest for the company's vice presidency, George still has trouble making it to work on time and is often ratted on by tattletale robots. Most of his family vacations are interrupted by Spacely via visaphone, though, and he often has to work overtime and weekends.

While at work, George spends time with his office computer RUDI (Referential Universal Digital Indexer), which has a human personality.

Spacely Space Sprockets vs. Cogswell Cogs

Two companies in a constant battle for dominance. Two CEOs who will stop at nothing to outdo each other. A space-age rivalry like no other. The never-ending battle between Spacely Space Sprockets and Cogswell Cogs (and their competitive presidents) always manages to throw the characters in *The Jetsons* into unpredictable and uproarious situations. Price undercutting, employee theft, and corporate espionage are but a few of the tactics the companies have resorted to over the years.

"Test Pilot"

Cosmo S. Spacely

Mr. Spacely, the loud, blustery, diminutive president of Spacely Space Sprockets, tends to use excessive volume in his voice to compensate for his modest height.

Spacely (originally voiced by Mel Blanc) struggles constantly to accomplish just one goal: beat his competitor, Cogswell. He will do whatever is necessary to be more successful than his archrival. In his quest for space supremacy, Spacely will cajole George into being a guinea pig or scapegoat, and he can always get George to do what he wants by promising a promotion to vice president. However, Spacely's pledge usually vanishes when either he gets George to do what he wants or George messes up his assignment.

Although Spacely seems to tyrannize George, he takes the opposite tact with his wife, Stella, nearly always standing (or kneeling) in her presence, primed for groveling.

Arthur Spacely

Cosmo and Stella Spacely's chubby and mild-mannered son—who is in the same Space Cub troop as Elroy—is a well-adjusted kid despite his parents' overbearing personalities.

"Jetsons Night Out"

"Elroy's TV Show"

"Elroy's TV Show"

"Jetsons Night Out"

 Q WHAT IS THE NAME OF ARTHUR SPACELY'S DOG?

A ZERO

Stella Spacely

Cosmo Spacely's wife, Stella, is an intimidating woman fond of harassing her husband via visaphone while he is at the office. A fluttering socialite, she constantly badgers her husband to become involved with her plans. In an ironic twist (considering her thorny nature), Spacely timidly calls Stella his "Petunia," and nearly always accommodates her wishes.

"The Flying Suit"

"Uniblab"

"The Flying Suit"   "The Flying Suit"

H. G. Cogswell

Cogswell, the calculating, underhanded, cigar-chomping president of Cogswell Cogs and Spacely's much taller rival, lives to surpass Spacely and Spacely Space Sprockets in every facet of corporate life. He also loves to flick the ashes from his soggy space cigar onto Spacely's balding head.

Like Spacely, Cogswell will push his factory and his employees as far as it takes to win the many knock-down, drag-out fights between the two businesses. And like his pudgy peer, Cogswell will beg for leniency the moment he thinks he has been outdone.

Q WHAT COUNTRY CLUB DO BOTH SPACELY AND COGSWELL BELONG TO?

A THE MOONSIDE COUNTRY CLUB

CUTTING-EDGE TECHNOLOGY

Machines of the Future

Just as the Flintstones's hometown of Bedrock had numerous labor-saving machines powered by prehistoric creatures, the world of *The Jetsons* was concocted as a veritable futuristic utopia in terms of gadgetry and convenience.

Jane may moan that she is "nothing but a drudge," but the audience sees that most of her "housework" involves pushing buttons. In one memorable scene, her robot vacuum even brings her a hot cup of coffee while cleaning the floors. Jane has to watch the device, however, lest it cheat by sweeping crumbs under the rug.

Pushing buttons isn't always a walk in the park, however. Jane, tasked with doing so for the entire family, actually gets buttonitus, an affliction affecting fingers and one's mental state. And video exercising still requires a certain amount of physical exertion.

One of the most interesting aspects about the far-out technology on *The Jetsons* is how, since the program's inception, many of their predicted gadgets have actually been invented: The visaphone, the televiewer, and the robotic vacuum all have real-world twenty-first-century counterparts.

VISAPHONE
A video telephone and intercom featured in several episodes.

Communication

ELECTRONIC SNOOP

A flying photo-robot at Spacely Space Sprockets that snaps an instant picture of George changing the hands of the time clock in "Jetsons Night Out." It then flies into Spacely's office to display the evidence of George's tardiness and his duplicity.

3-D TV
An option on the Jetsons's TV that, with the push of a button, allows viewers to project people on TV, at life size, into the room. Elroy uses it in "Elroy's Pal."

TELEVIEWER
A device that allows the user to scan the newspaper on-screen. The gadget, seen in "Jetsons Night Out," features options that let the viewer see headlines, then read a complete article if they want more information.

X-1500 FLYING SUIT

Invented by Cogswell Cogs' researcher Moonstone in the episode "The Flying Suit," this device allows its wearer to fly via brainwaves.

SLIDEWALK

A moving sidewalk that makes an appearance in many episodes.

CARRY BELT

An antigravity belt pedestrians use to get around, which Judy wears in "Rosey's Boyfriend."

Transportation

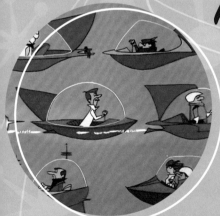

CAPSULE CAR

A flying car that is the standard mode of transportation in the *Jetsons* universe. George pilots his capsule car through traffic during the opening sequence of every episode.

FUEL PELLETS

The form of fuel for capsule cars. George stops to have some put in his tank in "Jetsons Night Out."

SPACEBOARD

Part skateboard, part surfboard, part hovercraft: Judy space-skis to school on one when a friend tows her behind his capsule car in "Elroy's Mob."

ELECTRONIC–BRAIN MOP

An automatic robot mop with bucket which cleans in the episode "The Space Car."

VACUUM ROBOT

As seen in "Miss Solar System," a device (not too far off from a certain actual modern vacuum cleaner) that cleans with the push of a button. In addition, the vacuum will bring its operator a drink (sadly the real life version has yet to provide that service).

EJECTOR MACHINE

A console in the Jetsons's home that, with the push of a button and a turn of the dial, ejects toast, records, or people. Jane uses it to eject George from bed in "Rosey the Robot."

Domestic Conveniences

RETRACTABLE BED

A bed that, at the push of a button, slides back and disappears into the wall. Elroy lies on one in "Dude Planet."

LAUNDRAGETTE

A Jetson home appliance that washes, presses, folds, and sews clothes in "The Good Little Scouts."

FOODARACKACYCLE/ FOODOMAT/ MENULATOR

Different models of a home appliance that prepares meals at the push of a few buttons. As seen in the first *Jetson* episode, "Rosey the Robot," and many others throughout the series.

INSTANT-TAN MACHINE

With Miami, Honolulu, or Riviera settings. As seen in "Millionaire Astro."

MORNING MASK

In the morning during the episode "The Space Car," when Jane considers herself too unpresentable to answer the visaphone, she slips this mask on, which temporarily gives her a made-up face and styled hair.

VIDEO EXERCISE

While still lying in bed in the episode "Uniblab," George watches a video of himself exercising. Apparently, it is enough to make him work up a sweat.

INSTANT RAINCOAT

Sprayed on from a canister, this transparent, bubble-like full-body covering leaves a hole for the wearer's face and gives complete weather protection. Elroy dons his in "Jetsons Night Out."

Health, Beauty, and Grooming

DRESS SELECTOR

A device that allows Jane to see how a dress will fit her by projecting an image of the dress on her body. She uses it to get dressed up in "Private Property."

SUPERSONIC DRESS-O-MATIC

A slide-through machine that dresses the person filing through. When George goes through in "Uniblab," he accidentally comes out wearing women's clothes.

DOG BATH-A-MAT

A contraption that grabs Astro and places him in an enclosed, see-through, automatic dog bath in "TV or Not TV."

MAGNO-MANICURE

A home beauty tool that gives Judy an instant manicure in "TV or Not TV."

FAVORITE EPISODES, SPECIALS, AND THE BIG SCREEN

A DATE WITH JET SCREAMER

This, only the second *Jetsons* episode produced, remains a fan favorite. It begins with George getting a speeding ticket, and the cop remarking that George must have thought he was racing in the Indianapolis 500,000.

The episode continues with Judy and her friends dancing, literally, in midair (with the aid of an antigravity floor) to the "Solar Swivel." We meet Jet Screamer—pop star, teen idol, and major crush of Judy's—whose signature phrase is "Baby, baby, baby, ah ah ah ah."

Judy then announces that she is entering a songwriting contest to win the grand prize: a date with Jet himself. Her inspired lyrics include "I want to run barefoot through your long black hair." Later, Elroy shows his dad a piece of paper with a secret code he has been working on with

Q ACCORDING TO THE SONG JET SCREAMER WROTE USING JUDY (AND ELROY'S) LYRICS, "EEP-OPP-ORK-AH-AH" MEANS "I LOVE YOU." BUT WHAT WAS THE CODE ORIGINALLY SUPPOSED TO MEAN?

A "MEET ME TONIGHT"

"Baby, baby, baby, ah ah ah ah!" —JET SCREAMER

a friend (and with Judy, we later learn). One of the code phrases is "Eep-opp-ork-ah-ah."

George, not wanting Judy to win the contest because he despises Jet's music, decides to mail Elroy's code instead of her song lyrics. But he gets his comeuppance when his daughter wins the contest anyway, and the family is instantly interviewed by a TV camera crew.

Ever the protective father, George decides to follow Judy and Jet on their date, hilariously mishearing several pieces of their conversation and interpreting them in the worst possible light. Eventually, they get to the set of Jet's TV show, where George bribes Jet's drummer ten dollars to

let him sit in. A memorable musical interlude follows where we see George as a very talented drummer, get to hear the catchy "Eep-opp-ork-ah-ah" song, and watch a spacey animation sequence that resembles a music video. George is won over by the end of the episode, and becomes the president of Jet Screamer's fan club.

"A Date with Jet Screamer" is irresistible from beginning to end and has one of the best plots and most memorable guest stars (Howard Morris) of the whole series. But one question remains: If George is that talented a drummer, why on earth is he working for Mr. Spacely?

"Eep-opp-ork-ah-ah means that I love you."

—JET SCREAMER

Q WHEN GEORGE GETS THE SPEEDING TICKET, HOW FAST DOES THE COP SAY HE WAS GOING?

A 3,500 MPH IN A 2,500 ZONE

MISS SOLAR SYSTEM

This delightful romp, which provides some very sweet moments between George and Jane, begins with Jane buying a new outfit and getting her feelings hurt when George is too distracted to notice it. He is, in fact, utterly transfixed by TV personality Gina Lollajupiter and her announcement about the upcoming Miss Solar System pageant—the chief sponsor of which is Spacely Space Sprockets.

After seeing Jane upset, her friend Gloria suggests that Jane enter the contest to teach George a lesson. Jane sends in a comely picture of herself wearing a masquerade outfit to the pageant organizers. After complaining about her domestic drudgery to the robotic vacuum, Jane gets a pleasant surprise when the pageant committee asks her to be a contestant.

Meanwhile, Spacely is set to serve as judge (wearing a mask so his wife won't recognize him). Unbeknownst to Jane, Spacely invites George along for the ride. However, when Stella Spacely, seeing right through her husband's

Q WHO DESIGNED THE GREEN GOWN JANE WEARS IN THE BEGINNING OF THE EPISODE?

A PIERRE MARTIAN

MISS SATURN

Literary-minded Miss Saturn does a reading of "Twinkle, Twinkle Little Star" for the talent portion of the event.

MISS MARS

For her talent, Miss Mars performs "The Galaxy Concerto" by Irving Galaxy, playing the saxophone, drums, and cymbals simultaneously.

MISS BIG DIPPER

We never get to see Miss Big Dipper's talent competition, but she certainly knows how to make an entrance.

"I'm just a drudge, that's all I am — an underpaid drudge!" —JANE JETSON

disguise, recognizes him, George is left to wear the mask and judge the contest alone.

The solar system's most memorable women are introduced by emcee Fred Solarvan, including Miss Saturn, Miss Mars, Miss Big Dipper, and the masked Miss Western Hemisphere. After a rousing rendition of "Won't You Fly Home, Bill Spacely" by Miss Western Hemisphere, George droolingly names her the winner.

When the new Miss Solar System removes her mask, George is shocked to find out he has been watching Jane all along. Naturally, Jane is disqualified for being married to the judge, but that doesn't matter a bit to the happy couple. Romance is rekindled for the Jetsons , and all's well that ends well.

"Crown or no crown, you'll always be my beauty queen. —GEORGE JETSON

MISS WESTERN HEMISPHERE

The talented Miss Western Hemisphere creates "planetary pandemonium" when she performs an "old American folk ballad." The jazzy rendition of "Won't You Fly Home, Bill Spacely" has the crowd (and George) clamoring for an encore.

TV SPECIALS AND THE BIG SCREEN

The Jetsons Meet the Flintstones

The third season of *The Jetsons* ended with a particularly special feature-length TV movie in which the space age family encountered their Stone Age counterparts, the Flintstones.

The Jetsons Meet the Flintstones (1987) saw the futuristic family propelled back in time thanks to a time machine created by Elroy. They had intended to take a break in the twenty-fifth century, but Astro accidentally knocked the controls to the "Past" setting, transporting the Jetsons to Bedrock. After getting over the initial shock and meeting the Flintstones, the Jetsons help the just-fired Fred and Barney get their jobs back and save the quarry from a hostile takeover.

Rockin' with Judy Jetson

The year after *The Jetsons Meet the Flintstones*, Judy Jetson took center stage in the space-age family's next feature-length TV movie, *Rockin' with Judy Jetson*. Sadly, it was the last *Jetsons* project to feature the entire original voice cast.

In the film, Judy falls head over heels for Sky Rocker, the latest hip rock star she has her eye on. As she did with Jet Screamer, she writes Sky a song, hoping to get his attention. Sky, however, loses the song when he bumps into Quark and Quasar, two cronies who work for the nefarious Felonia Funk, a villainess who hates music and has plans to obtain a rare diamond that will help her destroy music forever.

While Quark and Quasar walk away from their run-in with Sky carrying Judy's song, Sky ends up with the message they were carrying for Felonia. Soon, he's singing her secret plans on the airwaves. Due to this mix up, Felonia targets Sky, and Judy and her friends must rush to his rescue!

Jetsons: The Movie

It wasn't until summer 1990, with the release of *Jetsons: The Movie*, that the Jetsons finally made the jump to the big screen. Directed by Bill Hanna and Joe Barbera (along with famed illustrator Iwao Takamoto), the movie marked the final performances of George O'Hanlon (the voice of George Jetson) and Mel Blanc (the voice of Cosmo Spacely). To the dismay of fans, Judy Jetson was voiced by pop singer Tiffany rather than by original cast member Janet Waldo.

The film saw George finally achieve his professional dream of becoming vice president of Spacely Space Sprockets and moving with his family to oversee work at Spacely's Orbiting Ore Asteroid. But knowing Spacely, there had to be a catch! Turns out that four vice presidents have already come and gone. At the heart of the problem is an alien race called the Grungees whose home at the center of the asteroid is being harmed. It is up to George to find a solution that will save the Grungees' world without incurring Spacely's wrath.

POP-CULTURE FAMILY

The vinyl head of a vintage George Jetson
hand puppet by Knickerbocker.

Books, Games, Toys, and More . . .

It seems only natural that a world as fun as *The Jetsons* would spawn a google of spacey accessories. All types of *Jetsons* products have been sold ever since the first season, including coloring books, comic books, story books, figurines, puppets, puzzles, wind-up toys, board games, video games, costumes, lunch boxes, and stickers.

The long list of *Jetsons* merchandise, along with the show's ongoing syndication, has kept the futuristic family alive in the popular imagination.

▲ *A year after their first season, the Jetsons family was featured in a 35-issue series of comic books by Gold Key Comics. Archie, DC, and Harvey Comics subsequentley published their own limited series of Jetsons comics.*

LUNCH BOX BOTTOM

LUNCH BOX SIDE

▲ *A plastic tile sliding-square game in which several different picture combinations could be created, lining up the four main Jetson family members next to each other.*

◀ *The lunch box of the future! Made by Aladdin Enterprises in 1963. The colorful design shows the family riding in capsule cars and communicating via visaphone. Even the bottom is decorated with an image of the Jetsons around the Menulator. Lunch was complete with the addition of a steel thermos.*

▼ *Vintage mechanical wind-up toys made by Marx.*

◀ A page from a Gold Key Jetsons comic book in which George finds a unique way to roast a marshmallow.

▼ (clockwise from right) A Jetsons coloring book by Whitman Publishing; Gold Key's Jetsons comic #32; and a cut-out book of paper dolls, also by Whitman.

▲ Other fun vintage Jetsons toys include a rubber-band-powered "space copter" made by Transogram and a rolling Astro toy with "friction drive" by Marx.

◀ Collectible figurines of George, Jane, and Judy Jetson.

Credits

ACKNOWLEDGMENTS

Insight Editions would like to thank the following people for making this book possible: Greg Jones at Running Press; Victoria Selover, Melanie Swartz, Elaine Piechowski, and Mark Greenhalgh at Warner Bros.; Jonathan Cobin and Sandee Gold; and Lucy Kee, Mark Burstein, Mark Nichol, and Jan Hughes.

And special thanks to the following galleries, which opened their doors and made art available for this publication:

THE CARTOON ART MUSEUM
www.cartoonart.org

CLAMPETT STUDIO COLLECTIONS
www.clampettstudio.com

GREAT AMERICAN INK
www.cartoongallery.com

HERITAGE AUCTIONS
www.ha.com

HOUSE OF ANIMATION
(818) 812-9682

VAN EATON GALLERIES
www.vegalleries.com

WONDERFUL WORLD OF ANIMATION
www.animationartgallery.com

ISBN-13: 978-0-7624-4084-9
Library of Congress Control Number 2010937316

INSIGHT EDITIONS
An Insight Editions Book
www.insighteditions.com

Designed by Michel Vrána

Running Press Book Publishers
2300 Chestnut St.
Philadelphia, PA 19103

Visit us on the web!
www.runningpress.com

Manufactured in China by Insight Editions